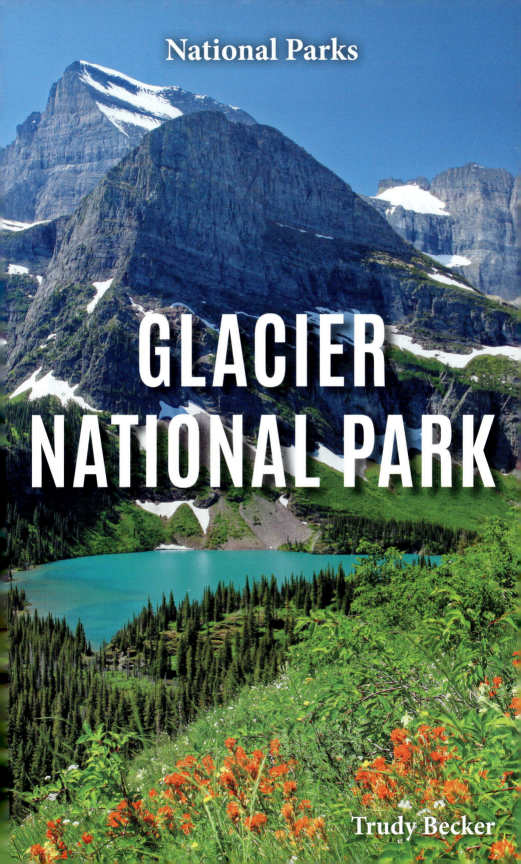

WWW.APEXEDITIONS.COM

Copyright © 2025 by Apex Editions, Mendota Heights, MN 55120. All rights reserved. No part of this book may be reproduced or utilized in any form or by any means without written permission from the publisher.

Apex is distributed by North Star Editions:
sales@northstareditions.com | 888-417-0195

Produced for Apex by Red Line Editorial.

Photographs ©: Shutterstock Images, cover, 1, 4–5, 6–7, 8–9, 10–11, 12–13, 14–15, 18–19, 30–31, 32–33, 34–35, 36–37, 40–41, 42–43, 46–47, 48–49, 52–53, 54–55, 56–57; Red Line Editorial, 16–17, 29, 44–45, 58; Bettmann/Getty Images, 20–21; John C. H. Grabill/Heritage Art/Heritage Images/Hulton Archive/Getty Images, 22–23; Brandstaetter Images/Imagno/Hulton Archive/Getty Images, 24–25; David Goldman/AP Images, 26–27; Beth J. Harpaz/AP Images, 39; Chris Jordan/Daily Inter Lake/AP Images, 50–51; National Park Service, 58–59

Library of Congress Control Number: 2024942978

ISBN
979-8-89250-453-9 (hardcover)
979-8-89250-469-0 (paperback)
979-8-89250-500-0 (ebook pdf)
979-8-89250-485-0 (hosted ebook)

Printed in the United States of America
Mankato, MN
012025

NOTE TO PARENTS AND EDUCATORS

Apex books are designed to build literacy skills in striving readers. Exciting, high-interest content attracts and holds readers' attention. The text is carefully leveled to allow students to achieve success quickly.

TABLE OF CONTENTS

Chapter 1
ICE IN THE HEAT 4

Chapter 2
ALL ABOUT GLACIER 8

Chapter 3
PEOPLE AND THE GLACIERS 18

Natural Wonder
TRIPLE DIVIDE 28

Chapter 4
HAVING FUN AT GLACIER 31

Natural Wonder
GRINNELL GLACIER 38

Chapter 5
WILDLIFE 41

Chapter 6
SAVING THE PARK 50

PARK MAP • 58
COMPREHENSION QUESTIONS • 60
GLOSSARY • 62
TO LEARN MORE • 63
ABOUT THE AUTHOR • 63
INDEX • 64

Chapter 1
ICE IN THE HEAT

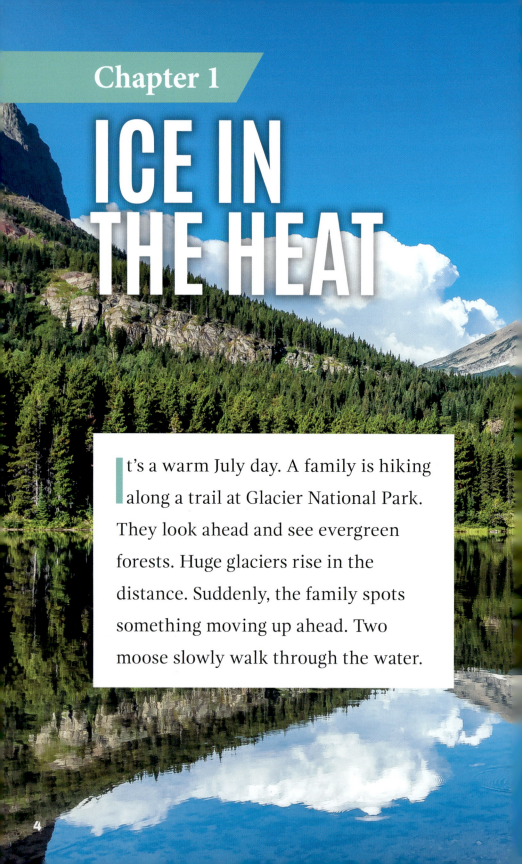

It's a warm July day. A family is hiking along a trail at Glacier National Park. They look ahead and see evergreen forests. Huge glaciers rise in the distance. Suddenly, the family spots something moving up ahead. Two moose slowly walk through the water.

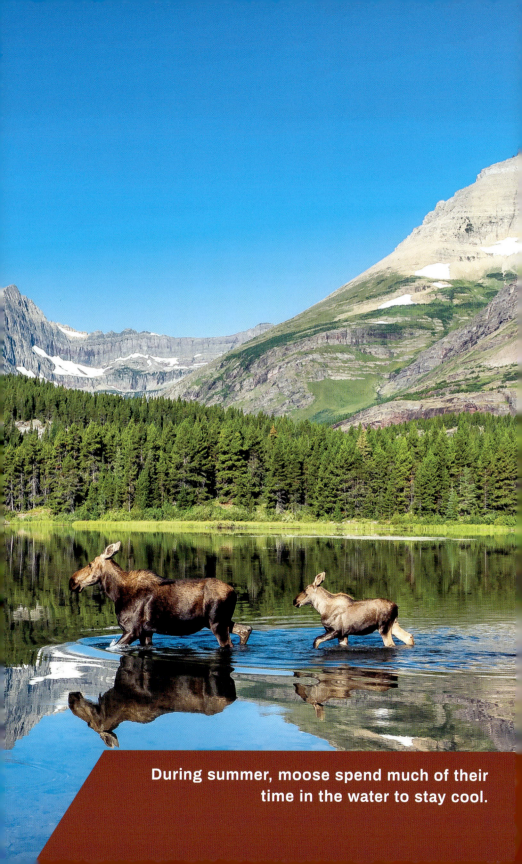
During summer, moose spend much of their time in the water to stay cool.

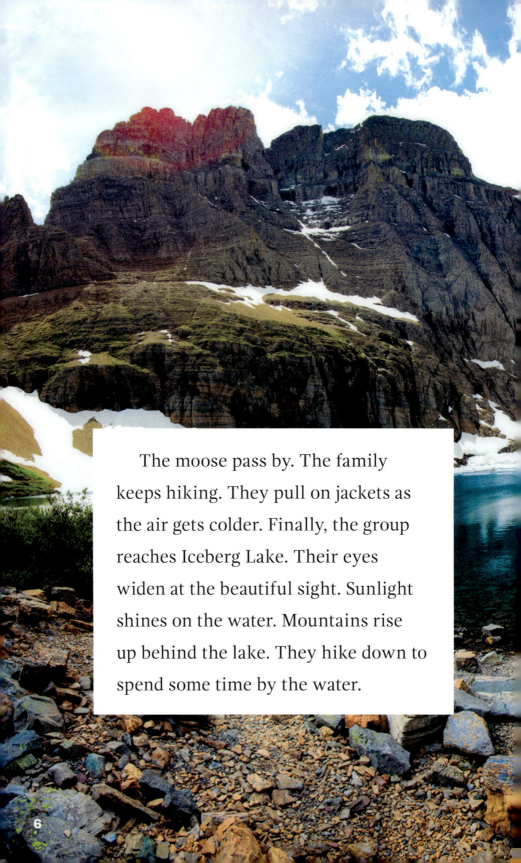

The moose pass by. The family keeps hiking. They pull on jackets as the air gets colder. Finally, the group reaches Iceberg Lake. Their eyes widen at the beautiful sight. Sunlight shines on the water. Mountains rise up behind the lake. They hike down to spend some time by the water.

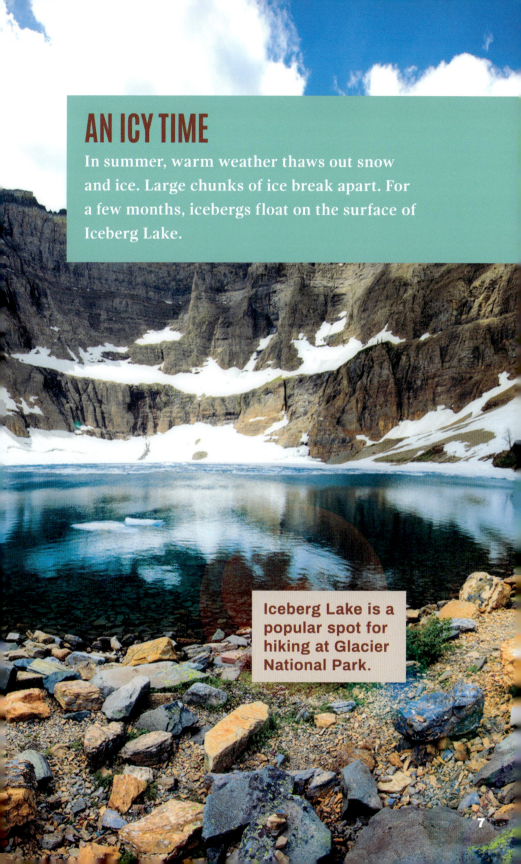

AN ICY TIME

In summer, warm weather thaws out snow and ice. Large chunks of ice break apart. For a few months, icebergs float on the surface of Iceberg Lake.

Iceberg Lake is a popular spot for hiking at Glacier National Park.

Chapter 2
ALL ABOUT GLACIER

Glacier National Park is in Montana. The park is huge. It covers more than 1,500 square miles (4,000 sq km). That is bigger than the state of Rhode Island. The park is named for its glaciers. They are the area's most famous feature.

Glacier National Park is the 12th-largest national park in the United States.

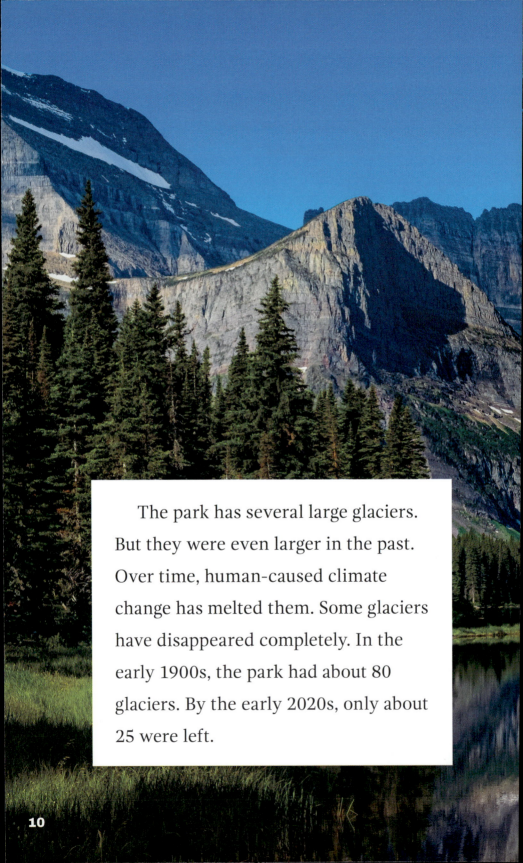

The park has several large glaciers. But they were even larger in the past. Over time, human-caused climate change has melted them. Some glaciers have disappeared completely. In the early 1900s, the park had about 80 glaciers. By the early 2020s, only about 25 were left.

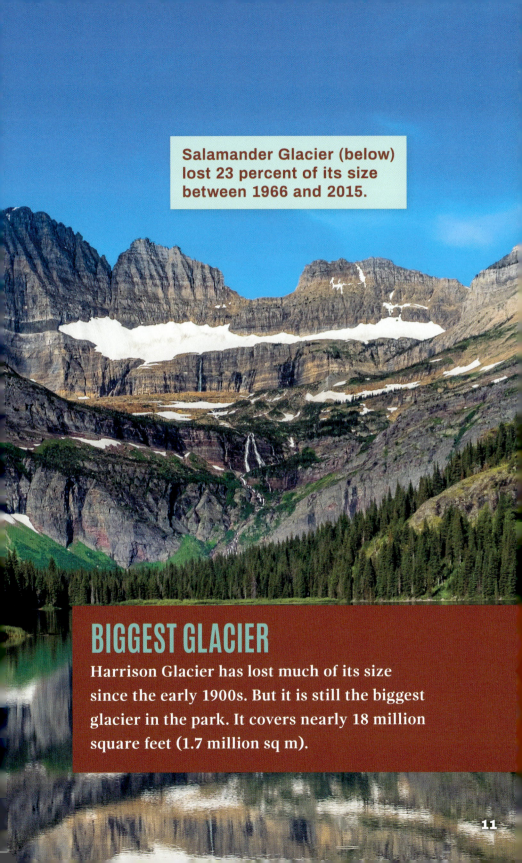

Salamander Glacier (below) lost 23 percent of its size between 1966 and 2015.

BIGGEST GLACIER

Harrison Glacier has lost much of its size since the early 1900s. But it is still the biggest glacier in the park. It covers nearly 18 million square feet (1.7 million sq m).

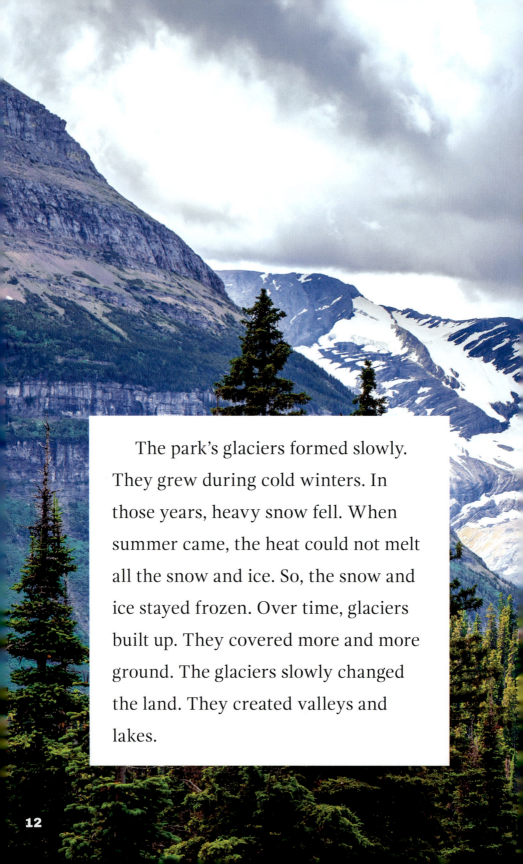

The park's glaciers formed slowly. They grew during cold winters. In those years, heavy snow fell. When summer came, the heat could not melt all the snow and ice. So, the snow and ice stayed frozen. Over time, glaciers built up. They covered more and more ground. The glaciers slowly changed the land. They created valleys and lakes.

The weight of a glacier's ice makes the glacier slide across the land over thousands of years.

Glacier National Park is known as the "Crown of the Continent."

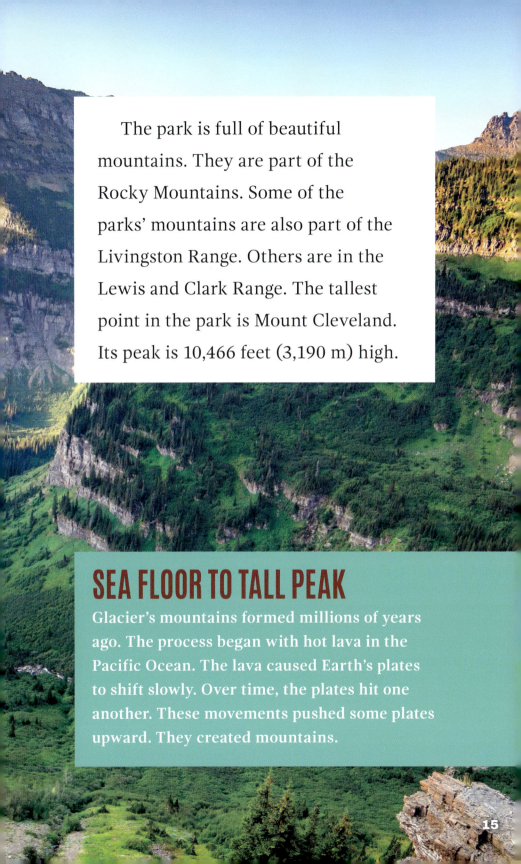

The park is full of beautiful mountains. They are part of the Rocky Mountains. Some of the parks' mountains are also part of the Livingston Range. Others are in the Lewis and Clark Range. The tallest point in the park is Mount Cleveland. Its peak is 10,466 feet (3,190 m) high.

SEA FLOOR TO TALL PEAK

Glacier's mountains formed millions of years ago. The process began with hot lava in the Pacific Ocean. The lava caused Earth's plates to shift slowly. Over time, the plates hit one another. These movements pushed some plates upward. They created mountains.

Water is a key part of Glacier's landscape. Waterfalls splash down the mountains. The park also has more than 700 lakes. Lake McDonald is the most famous. The lake is 10 miles (16 km) long. Many people visit it. Hidden Lake is another well-known site. Visitors can spot it from Hidden Lake Overlook.

OLD, ICY LAKES

Glacier's lakes formed long ago. They were created during the Ice Age. During that time, the glaciers moved. Some of them melted. Water filled the holes they left behind.

Many visitors drive past Saint Mary Lake while visiting Glacier.

17

Chapter 3

PEOPLE AND THE GLACIERS

Humans have lived in the area for at least 10,000 years. The earliest people were Indigenous groups. The Blackfeet people made their homes in the area. So did the Salish and Kootenai peoples. These groups used the land to hunt and gather food. Some believed the land was sacred.

Bison were an important food source for many Indigenous peoples.

In the 1700s, white settlers arrived. They began oppressing Indigenous groups. In 1855, the US government and the Blackfeet signed a treaty. It set aside land for the tribes. But settlers had destroyed the tribes' food sources. Many Indigenous people faced hunger and poverty. So, in 1895, they sold some land to the United States.

TERROR AT MARIAS

The Blackfeet and the US government often fought. In 1870, US soldiers found a group of Blackfeet near the Marias River. US soldiers killed more than 170 people. Most were women and children.

Blackfeet people set up tepees along the shore of Two Medicine Lake in the early 1900s.

In the 1800s, more and more white settlers moved into the area. Many wanted beaver pelts. They hoped to sell the pelts for money. Other people came for mining. They wanted to dig for gold and copper. The crowds of settlers did not stop.

Miners and other settlers helped Montana's population increase quickly in the 1800s.

RIDING THE RAILS

In 1891, workers finished the Great Northern Railway. The railroad helped people send their goods to other parts of the country. But it also helped more settlers arrive. They made homes in the area.

Glacier National Park was the country's eighth national park.

As more settlers arrived, some started to worry about nature. George Bird Grinnell was an explorer. He wanted to conserve the land. Grinnell and others wanted to create a national park. In 1910, their work paid off. President William Howard Taft signed a bill into law. Glacier National Park was created.

EARLY DAYS

At first, the park was very wild. The land was difficult to travel across. People created many trails. Some visitors hiked. Others rode horses. They had to move slowly.

Blackfeet people perform a dance in traditional clothing.

Over time, the park changed. People built more lodges for visitors to stay in. Park workers also developed more trails. They built roads, too. As a result, more and more visitors arrived. By the 2020s, millions of people came each year.

BLACKFEET LAND

The Blackfeet people still live near Glacier National Park. Many want to teach visitors about the land's history. So, some Blackfeet hope to create their own park nearby. That way, they could better protect the land. They could also earn more money for the tribe.

Natural Wonder

TRIPLE DIVIDE

Glacier National Park includes a continental divide. This is a raised area of land that separates water systems. Water on each side of the divide flows into different areas.

Most continental divides send water in two directions. But the divide at Glacier is different. It is a triple divide. Water flows into three different areas. In the southeast, water flows to the Gulf of Mexico. Water in the northeast goes to Hudson Bay. And in the west, water reaches the Pacific Ocean.

Glacier National Park has one of the only triple divides in North America.

On the Highline Trail, hikers must go up steep hills.

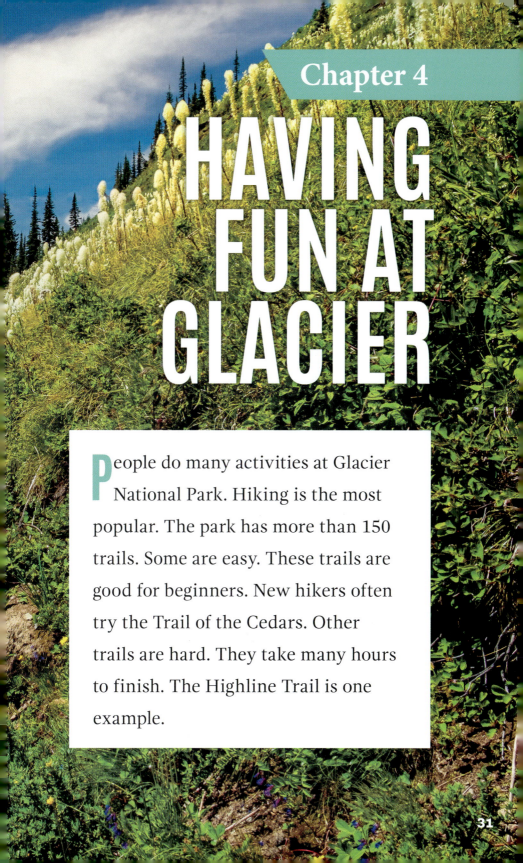

Chapter 4

HAVING FUN AT GLACIER

People do many activities at Glacier National Park. Hiking is the most popular. The park has more than 150 trails. Some are easy. These trails are good for beginners. New hikers often try the Trail of the Cedars. Other trails are hard. They take many hours to finish. The Highline Trail is one example.

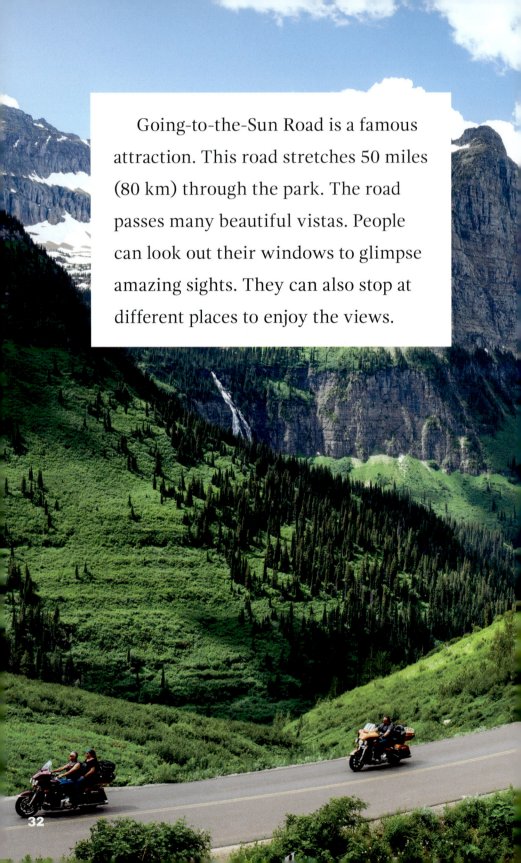

Going-to-the-Sun Road is a famous attraction. This road stretches 50 miles (80 km) through the park. The road passes many beautiful vistas. People can look out their windows to glimpse amazing sights. They can also stop at different places to enjoy the views.

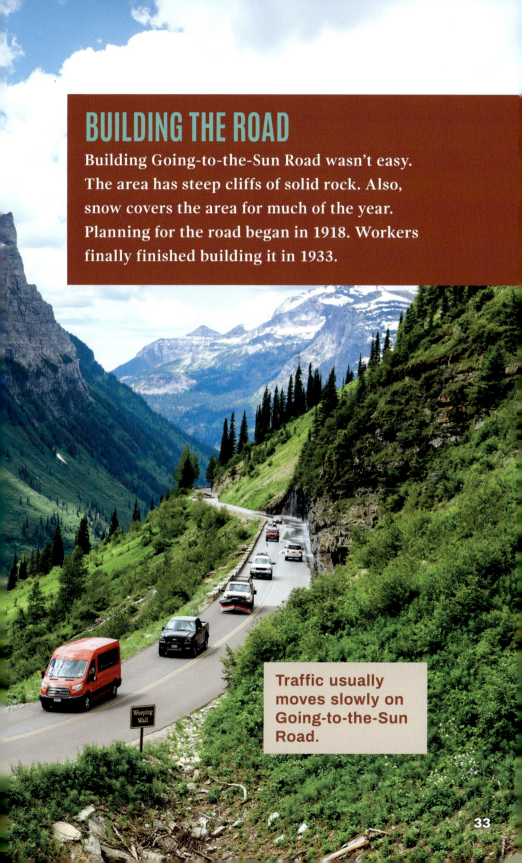

BUILDING THE ROAD

Building Going-to-the-Sun Road wasn't easy. The area has steep cliffs of solid rock. Also, snow covers the area for much of the year. Planning for the road began in 1918. Workers finally finished building it in 1933.

Traffic usually moves slowly on Going-to-the-Sun Road.

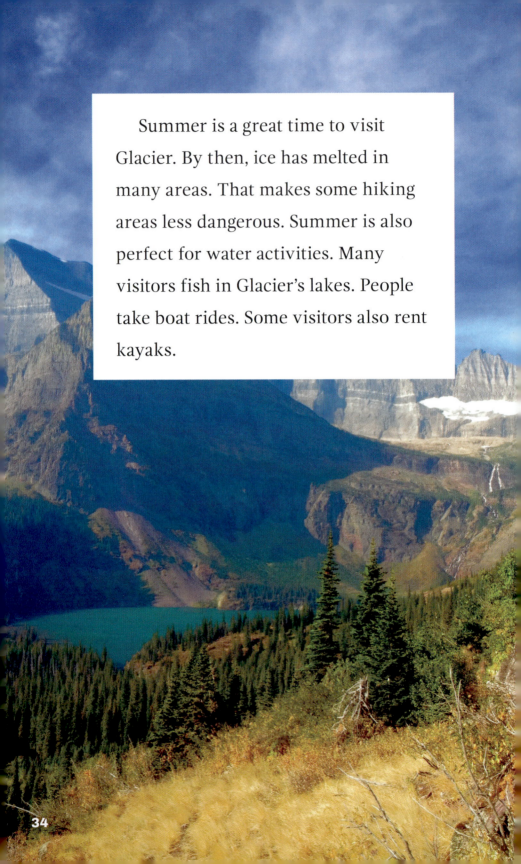

Summer is a great time to visit Glacier. By then, ice has melted in many areas. That makes some hiking areas less dangerous. Summer is also perfect for water activities. Many visitors fish in Glacier's lakes. People take boat rides. Some visitors also rent kayaks.

WHERE TO STAY

Visitors have many sleeping options. Some stay in the park's historic lodges. Others stay in campgrounds. Areas such as Kintla Lake are quiet and distant. St. Mary is closer to shops. Visitors can also stay in hotels outside the park.

Glacier National Park has more than 700 miles (1,100 km) of hiking trails.

Winter is another beautiful time in the park. Bright snow sparkles on the forests and mountains. Winter visitors can enjoy cross-country skiing. Visitors can also rent snowshoes. These are great ways to cross the park and see the sights.

WINTER SAFETY

Some areas are closed during winter. Snow and ice makes these places too dangerous. Visitors should always stay on marked paths. They should also wear warm clothes.

Hiking poles help people keep their balance in the snow.

Natural Wonder

GRINNELL GLACIER

Scientists believe the park's glaciers will be gone soon. It may happen by the 2030s. So, many visitors want to see the glaciers before they melt. Grinnell Glacier is one of the park's most famous glaciers. It is in Many Glacier Valley.

Visitors can reach Grinnell Glacier by hiking. Along the trail, hikers get great views of Grinnell Lake. Waterfalls tumble into the clear water. Around it, the glacier covers more than 100 acres (40 ha).

In 1850, Grinnell Glacier covered 710 acres (290 ha). It loses a few acres every year.

Elk are known for making loud, high-pitched noises that sound like screaming.

WILDLIFE

Glacier National Park has a strong, balanced ecosystem. The ecosystem includes many huge mammals. Visitors often spot bison and moose. These animals have thick layers of fat to stay warm in the winter. Elk are another common sight. They stay warm with their thick fur.

Glacier's most famous animals are bears. Two types of bear live in the park. Around 600 black bears wander the land. So do 300 grizzly bears. Bears are common across many parts of the park. Visitors see them most often in Many Glacier Valley.

BEAR SAFETY

Visitors must be very careful of bears. People should not get closer than 300 feet (90 m). Hikers should also carry bear spray. Making loud noises helps, too. That way, bears can hear hikers and stay away.

Grizzly bears can weigh more than 600 pounds (270 kg).

Logan Pass is a good place to see goats and sheep.

Mountain goats roam throughout the park. So do bighorn sheep. The icy habitat is perfect for these animals. Melting glaciers leave salt behind on the ground. Goats and sheep lick it up. These animals have features to survive the cold. For example, bighorn sheep have two thick layers of fur.

SMALL MAMMALS

Many small mammals live in the park. Some, such as rabbits and bats, are common across the United States. Others are more rare. Glacier is home to pygmy shrews and pikas.

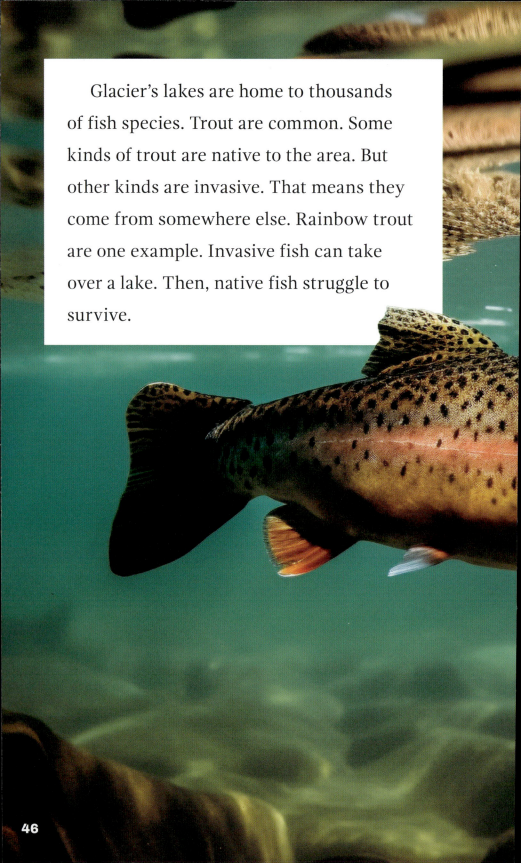

Glacier's lakes are home to thousands of fish species. Trout are common. Some kinds of trout are native to the area. But other kinds are invasive. That means they come from somewhere else. Rainbow trout are one example. Invasive fish can take over a lake. Then, native fish struggle to survive.

BIRDS BIG AND SMALL

Glacier is a great place for bird-watchers. The park's waters are home to several duck species. Bigger birds, such as osprey, also live there. And visitors often spot bald eagles.

Rainbow trout are known for the red stripes on their sides.

The Trail of the Cedars is a popular hiking area.

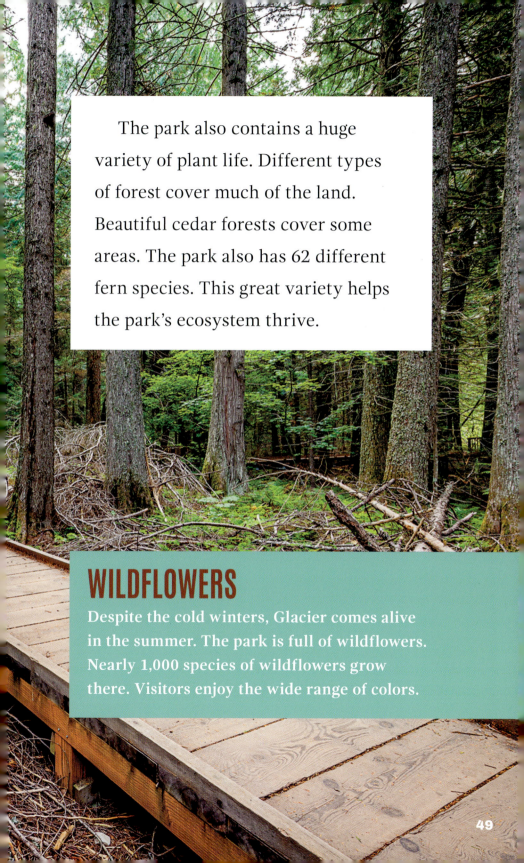

The park also contains a huge variety of plant life. Different types of forest cover much of the land. Beautiful cedar forests cover some areas. The park also has 62 different fern species. This great variety helps the park's ecosystem thrive.

WILDFLOWERS

Despite the cold winters, Glacier comes alive in the summer. The park is full of wildflowers. Nearly 1,000 species of wildflowers grow there. Visitors enjoy the wide range of colors.

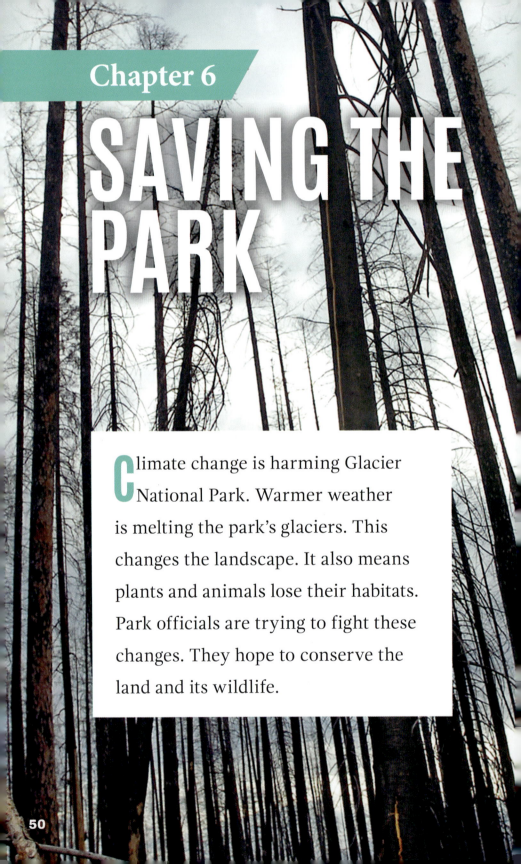

Chapter 6

SAVING THE PARK

Climate change is harming Glacier National Park. Warmer weather is melting the park's glaciers. This changes the landscape. It also means plants and animals lose their habitats. Park officials are trying to fight these changes. They hope to conserve the land and its wildlife.

Climate change is making wildfires larger and more common at Glacier National Park.

Some projects focus on species with low populations. Officials often bring more bison to the park when numbers are low. Other projects help more than one species at once. For example, officials re-plant whitebark pine trees. Clark's nutcrackers are birds that need those trees. With more whitebark pine, the park can support more of the birds.

TOO MANY MUSSELS

Mussels are shelled animals that live in water. They reproduce quickly. They can quickly take over bodies of water. So, Glacier's workers check all boats that arrive. They make sure people don't bring in any mussels.

Clark's nutcrackers eat the seeds of pine trees.

Pikas are similar to rabbits, but they have smaller ears.

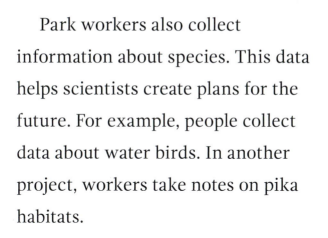

Park workers also collect information about species. This data helps scientists create plans for the future. For example, people collect data about water birds. In another project, workers take notes on pika habitats.

RARE PLANTS

Glacier is home to many rare plants. Several studies focus on conserving them. People observe plants in different areas. They look for changes and patterns. That helps scientists know what actions are needed.

Park operations are another key to conservation. Workers look for ways to use less energy. And they try to save water. Through these actions, the land and wildlife can keep thriving. And park visitors can continue enjoying Glacier National Park.

Visitor centers at Glacier National Park use solar panels to create electricity.

PARK MAP

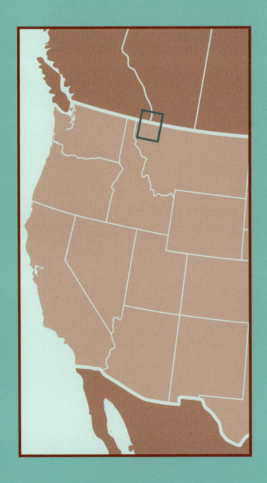
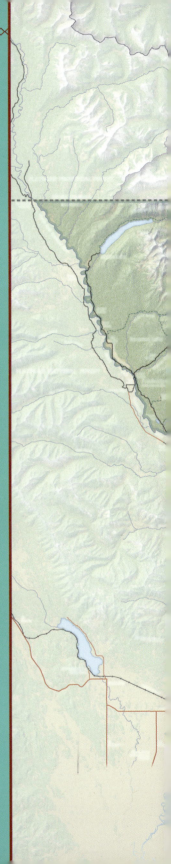

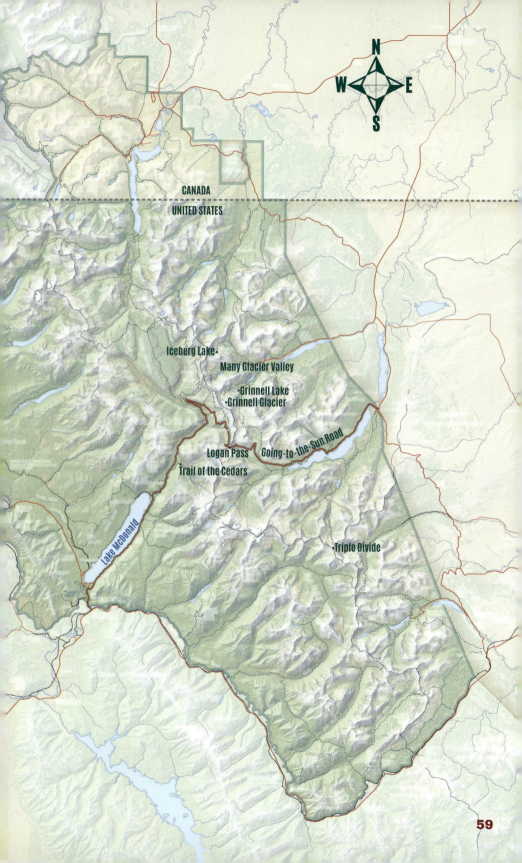

COMPREHENSION QUESTIONS

Write your answers on a separate piece of paper.

1. Write a paragraph describing the main ideas of Chapter 3.

2. What feature of Glacier National Park do you find most interesting? Why?

3. What animal is an invasive species in Glacier National Park?

    A. grizzly bear
    B. Clark's nutcracker
    C. rainbow trout

4. Why might melting glaciers harm some plants and animals in the park?

    A. All plants and animals need large glaciers to survive.
    B. Melting ice and warm weather could change the ecosystem.
    C. Many animals in the park live inside the ice.

5. What does **poverty** mean in this book?

*But settlers had destroyed the tribes' food sources. Many Indigenous people faced hunger and **poverty**. So, in 1895, they sold some land to the United States.*

    A. cooking fancy meals
    B. gaining money
    C. not having enough

6. What does **vistas** mean in this book?

*The road passes many beautiful **vistas**. People can look out their windows to glimpse amazing sights. They can also stop at different places to enjoy the views.*

    A. views of nature
    B. long, narrow roads
    C. cars full of people

Answer key on page 64.

GLOSSARY

climate change
A dangerous long-term change in Earth's temperature and weather patterns.

ecosystem
A group of living things and their environment.

glaciers
Large, slow-moving bodies of ice.

Indigenous
Related to the original people who lived in an area.

mammals
Animals that have hair and produce milk for their young.

operations
Actions taken to keep a park open for visitors.

oppressing
Treating people in a cruel or unfair way.

pelts
Animal skins with the fur still on.

plates
Huge pieces of Earth's crust that move and turn.

sacred
Having close ties to a god, goddess, or religion.

species
Groups of animals or plants that are similar and can breed with one another.

TO LEARN MORE

BOOKS

Bowman, Chris. *Glacier National Park*. Minneapolis: Bellwether Media, 2023.

Hamby, Rachel. *Grizzly Bears*. Mendota Heights, MN: Apex Editions, 2023.

Kington, Emily. *Climate Change*. Minneapolis: Lerner Publications, 2022.

ONLINE RESOURCES

Visit **www.apexeditions.com** to find links and resources related to this title.

ABOUT THE AUTHOR

Trudy Becker lives in Minneapolis, Minnesota. She hopes to visit Glacier National Park before the glaciers are gone.

INDEX

bears, 42
birds, 47, 52, 55
Blackfeet people, 18, 20, 27

climate change, 10, 50
conservation, 25, 50, 52, 55–56
continental divide, 28

fish, 34, 46

glaciers, 4, 8, 10–12, 16, 38, 45, 50
Going-to-the-Sun Road, 32–33
Grinnell, George Bird, 25

Harrison Glacier, 11
Hidden Lake, 16
hiking, 4, 6, 25, 31, 34, 38, 42

Ice Age, 16
Iceberg Lake, 6–7

Kootenai people, 18

Lake McDonald, 16

mining, 22
moose, 4, 6, 41
Mount Cleveland, 15
mussels, 52

pikas, 45, 55

railroads, 23
rainbow trout, 46
Rocky Mountains, 15

Salish people, 18
settlers, 20, 22–23, 25

Taft, William Howard, 25

waterfalls, 16, 38
wildflowers, 49

ANSWER KEY:
1. Answers will vary; 2. Answers will vary; 3. C; 4. B; 5. C; 6. A